The Authors

Jay McTighe directs the Maryland Assessment Consortium, a collaboration among Maryland's school systems to develop and share performance assessments with teachers throughout the state. He is well known for his work with "thinking skills," having coordinated statewide efforts to develop instructional strategies, curriculum models, and assessment procedures for improving the quality of student thinking.

Steven Ferrara is director of research and psychometrics at the American Institutes for Research in Washington, D.C. Formerly Maryland's State Director of Student Assessment, he has taught at the preschool, middle school, high school, and graduate levels. He has spent the last 12 years conducting research, writing, teaching, and speaking on the effects of large-scale and classroom assessment on teaching and learning.

Authors' Acknowledgments

The authors wish to thank the following individuals for their comments on and critique of various drafts of this document: Gail Goldberg, Joan Heiss, Mary Kimmins, Hillary Michaels, Ruth Mitchell, and Barbara Reeves. They also wish to thank the many users of the Framework of Assessment Approaches and Methods in an earlier version of this book for their helpful comments on using the Framework.

— J.M. and S.F.

Student Assessment Series

ASSESSING LEARNING IN THE CLASSROOM

Jay McTighe and Steven Ferrara

Glen W. Cutlip
Series Editor

nea
NATIONAL EDUCATION ASSOCIATION

Note

The opinions expressed in this publication should not be construed as representing the policy or position of the National Education Association. These materials are intended to be discussion documents for educators who are concerned with specialized interests of the profession.

Reproduction of any part of this book must include the usual credit line and copyright notice. Address communications to Editor, NEA Teaching and Learning.

Library of Congress Cataloguing-in-Publication Data
McTighe, Jay.
Assessing learning in the classroom / Jay McTighe and Steven Ferrara.
p. cm. — (Student assessment series)
Includes bibliographical references (p.).
ISBN 0-8106-2070-7
1. Achievement tests—United States. 2. Educational tests and measurements—United States. I. Ferrara, Steven. II. Title. III. Series.
LB3060.3.M38 1998   98-28469
371.27'1'0973—dc21   CIP

CONTENTS

INTRODUCTION

The field of student assessment—from methodology and techniques to the use of results—is changing, and these changes are dramatically affecting the work of education employees.

On one hand, these changes have created new options. For example, classroom assessment instruments have expanded to include assessments based on portfolios, projects, and performances. Teachers now assess a student's performance based on predetermined criteria more closely aligned with the instructional objectives of the lesson and tailor instruction more specifically to individual students. Students become partners with the teacher in assessment by having access to these criteria at the beginning of the lesson. Classroom assessment is truly becoming an integral part of the instructional program as more and more teachers add these assessment techniques to their repertoire.

On the other hand, changes in student assessment have created new concerns, especially in the use of assessment results. Today, assessment results are being used for more than comparing an individual student's performance against a state or national norm, and for more than providing data for making program improvement decisions. They are being used to determine the success or failure of teachers and schools. Policy makers and others are using large-scale assessments to decide whether teachers and schools are providing an adequate education to all students and attaching consequences, positive and negative, on the basis of student assessment results. The use of student test scores has raised the stakes for all education employees.

Consequently, student assessment is part of every teacher's work. In fact, nearly one-third of a classroom teacher's time is spent assessing and evaluating students. Many influential groups have identified competence in student assessment as essential for the training and licensing of new teachers and the upgrading of the skills of practicing teachers (National Board for Professional Teaching Standards, Interstate New Teacher Assessment Consortium, National Council for Accreditation of Teacher Education, Educational Testing Service, and the National Association of State Directors of Teacher Education and Certification). These groups estimate that less than one-half of currently practicing teachers have received adequate training in student assessment.

To help members and other educators keep abreast of the ever-changing field of student assessment, the National Education Association (NEA) commissioned leading assessment experts to write about student assessment from their perspectives. Experts Jay McTighe and Steven Ferrara, the authors of this book on classroom-based assessment of learning, believe that "the primary purpose of classroom assessment is to inform teaching and improve learning, not to sort and select students or to justify a grade." In this book, a revised edition of an NEA publication printed in 1994, they discuss principles of effective classroom assessment, illustrate a variety of assessment approaches and methods, and provide a framework for planning. Their readable, practical approach to an evolving and sometimes complex subject is intended to be of use to teachers at all levels, preschool through graduate studies, as well as to other education employees.

The NEA developed the Student Assessment Series to help teachers and other education employees improve their knowledge and skills in student assessment and hopes readers will find the series a valuable resource for current and future student assessment practices.

— Glen W. Cutlip
Series Editor

I.

ONGOING ASSESSMENT
OF STUDENT LEARNING

Ongoing assessment of student learning in the classroom is an essential aspect of effective teaching. Teachers can use a variety of assessment methods to diagnose students' strengths and needs, plan and adjust instruction, and provide feedback to students and parents regarding progress and achievement. The basic premise of this book is that the primary purpose of classroom assessment is to inform teaching and improve learning, not to sort and select students or to justify a grade.

The book is intended for teachers from the preschool to graduate school levels to use in examining a variety of methods for effectively and fairly assessing their students. While the choice of particular assessment methods will vary according to the purpose of the assessment, the content of the curriculum, and the age levels of students, a set of common principles underlies effective classroom assessment. This book covers these principles, provides the strengths and limitations of a variety of assessment approaches, presents a series of vignettes to illustrate classroom assessment in action, and offers a set of guiding questions and a framework for planning classroom assessments to improve teaching and learning.

> **The primary purpose of classroom assessment is to inform teaching and improve learning, not to sort and select students or to justify a grade.**

Teachers frequently begin new units of study by introducing or reviewing key vocabulary with the recognition that an understanding of certain basic concepts will enhance subsequent learning of important principles and procedures in the unit. Likewise, this book begins with a review of basic terminology commonly associated with classroom assessment. (Additional assessment terminology is provided throughout the book and definitions of related terms important to the topic of classroom assessment are provided in the Glossary.)

Assessment refers to "any systematic basis for making inferences about characteristics of people, usually based on various sources of evidence; the global process of synthesizing information about individuals in order to understand and describe them better" (Brown 1983). While considering this textbook definition, it is interesting to note that the term *assessment* is derived from the Latin root *assidere* meaning "to sit beside." Although this original meaning may seem at odds with present-day images of large-scale standardized testing—number 2 pencils, "bubble" sheets, rigid time limits, silent work, and so on—it conforms more closely with the array of assessment methods routinely used by teachers for assessing their students. *Assidere* suggests that, in addition to tests and projects, classroom assessments include informal methods of "sitting beside," observing, and conversing with students as a means of understanding and describing what they know and can do.

The terms *assessment, testing,* and *evaluation* are frequently used interchangeably, but they have distinct meanings. *Assessment* is a broad term referring to the process of gathering and synthesizing information to better understand and describe characteristics of people. *Testing* is one type of assessment. Tests generally utilize a paper-and-pencil format, are administered and

> **It is interesting to note that the term *assessment* is derived from the Latin root *assidere* meaning "to sit beside."**

taken within established time limits, restrict test takers' access to resources (e.g., reference materials), and yield a limited range of acceptable responses. *Evaluation* involves making a judgment regarding quality, value, or worth, based on set criteria. Teacher questioning, reviews of student work folders, and paper-and-pencil tests are commonly used assessment methods for gathering information about student learning. Scoring a student essay and assigning report card grades are examples of evaluation.

Another pair of widely used terms, *summative assessment* and *formative assessment,* pertain to the purpose and timing of classroom assessments. *Summative assessment* refers to any culminating assessment that provides a summary report on the degree of knowledge or proficiency attained at the conclusion of a unit, course, or program of study. A final exam, senior exhibition, or dissertation defense are examples of summative assessments. *Formative assessment* refers to any ongoing diagnostic assessment that provides information to help teachers adjust instruction and improve student performance. For instance, prior to the start of a unit on the Civil War, a teacher might ask students to make a "web" or an outline to show what they already know about this period of history as a means of obtaining information about students' prior knowledge. The teacher might also randomly select and interview several students to check their perceptions and awareness of the Civil War. Formative assessment also can be used during instruction to check on student understandings and misconceptions. Teachers often use brief written and oral quizzes and classroom discussions to determine if students have learned course material and can apply the skills they have been taught. Such activities provide teachers with valuable information that allows them to adjust instruction to improve student learning.

Although the term *alternative assessment* appears widely in the recent education literature (Herman, Aschbacher, and Winters 1992), there is no universally agreed-upon definition for the term *alternative*. Generally, *alternative assessment* is used to refer to those assessments that differ from the multiple-choice, timed, "one-shot" approaches that characterize most standardized and some classroom assessments. The term should be avoided as it is imprecise and open to various interpretations.

II.

LARGE-SCALE VERSUS CLASSROOM ASSESSMENT

Different types of assessments address different information needs. The purposes and audiences for assessment information influence what is assessed, how it is assessed, and how the results are communicated and used. Large-scale assessments have very specific purposes. For example, standardized tests, such as the Iowa Tests of Basic Skills (ITBS), California Achievement Tests (CAT), and the Stanford Achievement Test, are used primarily to satisfy the demands for educational accountability. The results of assessments such as these are reported to legislatures, boards of education, school administrators, parents, and the general public. Standardized tests are generally *norm referenced* to allow for easy interpretation. They are designed to determine how well students have learned particular concepts and skills as compared to other students in a norming group. The results of norm-referenced assessments may be conveniently displayed so that observers can readily distinguish achievement above or below the norm.

Not all large-scale standardized tests are norm referenced. Some, such as the College Board's Advanced Placement Examinations, the National Assessment of Educational Progress (NAEP), and certain state-level competency tests, are *criterion referenced*. These tests evaluate and report student performance compared to pre-established standards.

Furthermore, not all standardized tests are multiple-choice in nature. Several states currently use standardized performance assessments, featuring open-ended tasks, for "high stakes" accountability purposes.

Standardized tests are considered "high stakes tests" if their results are used for consequential decisions such as promotion, graduation, admission, certification, evaluation, or where rewards and sanctions are involved. For example, a districtwide minimum competency exam would be "high stakes" for students if passing the exam is a requirement for a high school diploma. For an extended discussion of standardized testing, see *The Role of High-Stakes Testing in School Reform* (Smith 1993). Because they are intended to provide accountability information, "one-shot" large-scale standardized tests typically do not provide sufficiently detailed or timely information regarding student achievement of specific curriculum goals.

Classroom assessments serve other purposes and audiences. At the classroom level, teachers have different assessment needs—diagnosing student strengths and weaknesses, informing students and parents about progress, planning and adjusting instruction, and motivating students to focus on valued knowledge and skills. With these purposes in mind, classroom assessments may be tailored directly to the curriculum and to the information needs of individual teachers, students, and parents. Unlike "one-shot" standardized tests, assessments designed to promote learning in the classroom are more likely to be used over time, include an array of methods, focus on elements of quality, offer a more personalized picture of student achievement, and provide timely and specific feedback.

III.

EFFECTIVE CLASSROOM ASSESSMENT

A large variety of methods is available to teachers for assessing student learning (Airasian 1991; Cross and Angelo 1988; Ferrara and McTighe 1992; Stiggins 1994). Regardless of the particular methods employed, effective classroom assessment is guided by three fundamental principles. Classroom assessment should: (1) inform teaching and improve learning; (2) use multiple sources of information; and (3) provide valid, reliable, and fair measurements.

The first principle is based on the premise that the primary purpose of classroom assessment is to inform teaching and improve learning (Mitchell and Neill 1992). Thus, effective classroom assessment must be an ongoing process instead of a single event at the conclusion of instruction. Rather than waiting until the end of a unit of study or course to assess students, effective teachers employ formative assessments at the beginning of instruction to determine students' prior knowledge, and they assess regularly throughout the unit or course of study to obtain information to help them adjust their teaching based on the learning needs of students. They recognize that assessment results can inform them about the effectiveness of their teaching as well as the degree of student learning.

> **Effective teachers employ formative assessments at the beginning of instruction ... and they assess regularly throughout the unit or course of study.**

When using performance-based assessments, teachers can make their evaluative criteria explicit in advance to serve as a focus for both instruction and evaluation. Effective teachers help their students understand that the criteria describe the desired elements of quality. They provide regular feedback to students based on the identified criteria and allow students to revise their work based upon this feedback. They also involve students in peer- and self-evaluation using the criteria in order to engage students more actively in improving their performance.

Assessment for learning recognizes the mutually supportive relationship between instruction and assessment. Like a Möbius strip where one side appears to seamlessly blend into the other, classroom assessment should reflect and promote good instruction. For example, teachers following a process approach to teaching writing would allow their students to develop drafts, receive feedback, and make revisions as part of the assessment. Likewise, if teachers teach science through a hands-on, experimental approach, their assessment should include hands-on investigations.

The second principle of sound classroom assessment calls for a synthesis of information from several sources. The importance of using multiple sources of information when assessing learning in the classroom can be illustrated through the analogy of taking photographs. A single assessment, such as a written test, is like a snapshot of student learning. While a snapshot is informative, it is generally incomplete since it portrays an individual at a single moment in time within a particular context. It is inappropriate to use one snapshot of student performance as the sole basis for drawing conclusions about how well a student has achieved desired learning outcomes. Classroom assessment offers a distinct advantage over a large-scale assessment in that it allows teachers to take frequent samplings of student learning using an array of methods. To continue the analogy of taking photographs, classroom assessment provides an opportunity to construct a "photo album" containing a variety of pictures taken at different times with different lenses, backgrounds, and compositions. The photo album reveals a richer, more complete picture of each student than any single snapshot can provide. Applying the principle of multiple sources is especially important when the assessment information is used as a basis for making critical summative decisions, such as assigning report card grades or determining promotion.

> **The principle of multiple sources is especially important when the assessment information is used as a basis for making critical summative decisions, such as assigning report card grades or determining promotion.**

The third principle of classroom assessment concerns validity, reliability, and fairness. *Validity* refers to the degree to which an assessment measures what it was intended to measure. For example, to assess students' abilities to conduct research using primary and secondary sources, a media specialist should observe students' use of these sources directly as they work on their research projects. For this learning outcome, a paper-and-pencil test of student knowledge of library references would be an indirect and less valid assessment since it does not reveal the ability to actually use the references purposefully.

Reliability refers to the dependability and consistency of assessment results. If the same assessment yielded markedly different results with the same students (without intervening variables such as extra instruction or practice time), one would question its reliability. Performance assessments present a special challenge since they call for judgment-based evaluation of student products and performances. A reliable evaluation would result in equivalent ratings by the same rater on different occasions. For instance, an observation checklist can be used reliably as long as teachers are careful to ensure that their ratings would not differ substantially from occasion to occasion (e.g., Monday morning versus Friday afternoon). When teachers are involved in school- or district-level evaluations based on a set of criteria used throughout the school or district, inter-rater reliability must also be considered. In this case, scores on a writing assessment would be considered reliable if different raters assign similar scores to the same essays.

Fairness in classroom assessment refers to giving all students an equal chance to show what they know and can do. Fairness is compromised when teachers assess something that has not been taught or use assessment methods that are incongruent with instruction (e.g., asking for recall of facts when the emphasis has been on reasoning and problem solving). The fairness of teacher judgments is also challenged by the "halo" and "pitchfork" effects, where expectations based on a student's past attitude, behavior, or previous performance influence the evaluation of his or her current performance.

Subtle, unintended racial, ethnic, religious, or gender biases also present roadblocks to the fair assessment of students. Such biases may negatively influence students' attitudes toward, and performances on, classroom assessments. For example, the junior high mathematics teacher who routinely uses sports statistics as a main source for problem-solving tasks could turn off those students who are not sports fans. Likewise, insensitivity to diverse religious beliefs (e.g., choosing reading passages involving only Christian holidays), gender/racial images (e.g., depicting all doctors as white males), or socioeconomic status (e.g., assuming that all kids have access to a telephone or home computer) may result in unfair evaluation of individuals or groups. Teachers must be on guard so that biases do not influence their evaluations of a student's performance.

> **Fairness is compromised when teachers assess something that has not been taught or use assessment methods that are incongruent with instruction.**

After teachers consider these three general principles, they should address some fundamental questions related to planning classroom assessments.

Content Standards, Purpose, and Audience

Just as teachers have numerous instructional techniques and strategies from which to choose, they also have a variety of methods available for assessing learning. Teachers can determine which assessment methods to use by responding to several key questions (see Figure 1).

The first question, under standards/benchmarks, concerns *content standards,* or the intended results of the teaching. Teachers should ask: "What do we want students to understand and be able to do?" Content standards typically fall into three categories: (1) *declarative knowledge*—what we want students to understand (facts, concepts, principles, generalizations); (2) *procedural knowledge*—what we want students to be able to do (skills, processes, strategies); and (3) *attitudes, values, or habits of mind*—how we would like students to be disposed to act (e.g., appreciate the arts, treat people with respect, avoid impulsive behavior). The choice of specific assessment methods should be determined in large part by the nature of the content standards being assessed (Marzano, Pickering, and McTighe 1993). For example, to assess students' ability to write an effective persuasive essay, the assessment should involve gathering samples of students' persuasive writing and evaluating them against specified criteria. In this case, a multiple-choice test would be ill-suited to measure the intended outcome. Likewise, to assess students' ability to work cooperatively on a research project, the assessment should assess group processes and products as well as individual performance.

In addition to considering content standards, teachers need to raise questions about the *purpose(s)* and *audience(s)* for classroom assessments. They should ask: "Why are we assessing and how will the assessment information be used? For whom are the assessment results intended?" Purpose and audience influence not only the assessment methods selected, but also the ways in which the results of classroom assessments are communicated. For example, to provide parents of a primary-grade student with an interim report of progress in language arts, the teacher might arrange a conference to describe the child's reading skills in terms of a developmental profile and review a work folder containing samples of the child's writing.

Figure 1

Classroom Assessment Planning: Key Questions

Standards/Benchmarks	Purpose(s) for Assessment	Audience(s) for Assessment
What do we want students to understand and be able to do?	*Why are we assessing and how will the assessment information be used?*	*For whom are the assessment results intended?*
☐ _____ _____ _____ _____ ☐ _____ _____ _____ _____ ☐ _____ _____ _____ _____	☐ Diagnose student strengths/ needs ☐ Provide feedback on student learning ☐ Provide a basis for instructional placement ☐ Inform and guide instruction ☐ Communicate learning expectations ☐ Motivate; focus student attention and effort ☐ Provide practice applying knowledge and skills ☐ Provide a basis for evaluation: ___ grading ___ promotion ___ program selection/ admissions ☐ Provide accountability data ☐ Gauge program effectiveness	☐ Teacher/ instructor ☐ Students ☐ Parents ☐ Grade-level/ department teams ☐ Other faculty ☐ School administrators ☐ Curriculum supervisors ☐ Business community/ employers ☐ College admissions officers ☐ Policy makers (e.g., board of education, state legislature) ☐ General public ☐ Other: _____

ples of widely used brief constructed-response methods. While brief constructed-response items may seek a correct or acceptable response (e.g., fill in the blank), they are more likely to yield a range of responses. Thus, the evaluation of student responses requires judgment, guided by criteria. This approach may be used for assessing declarative knowledge and procedural proficiency. In addition, assessments using brief constructed response items can provide insight into understanding and reasoning when students are requested to show their work and explain or defend their answers in writing.

Assessments using brief constructed-response items offer several advantages. They require less time to administer than other types of assessments using constructed-response formats. Since they elicit short responses, several brief constructed-response items may be used to assess multiple content standards. Evaluation of student responses is straightforward, guided by criteria and model responses.

Brief constructed-response items are limited in their ability to adequately assess attitudes, values, or habits of mind. In addition, they require judgment-based evaluation, which takes time and introduces potential problems of scoring reliability and fairness. Teachers are cautioned against regularly re-using brief constructed-response items for summative assessments so that students cannot give memorized responses to known questions and tasks.

Performance-Based Assessment

Performance-based assessments include student products, student performances, and process-focused assessments. Performance-based assessments require students to apply knowledge and skills rather than simply to recall and recognize. Thus, performance-based assessments are more likely to reveal student understanding. They are well suited to assessing application of content-specific knowledge, integration of knowledge across subject areas, and life-long learning competencies such as effective decision making, communication, and cooperation (Shepard 1989).

The current interest in performance-based methods has popularized additional assessment terms, such as *authentic assessment, rubric, anchors,* and *standards.* The term *authentic assessment,* popularized by Grant Wiggins (Wiggins 1989), is used to describe performance-based assessments that engage students in applying knowledge and skills in ways that they are used in the "real world." According to Wiggins, authentic assessments should also reflect good instructional practice in ways that

> **The term *authentic assessment* popularized by Grant Wiggins ... is used to describe performance-based assessments that engage students in applying knowledge and skills in ways that they are used in the "real world."**

make "teaching to the test" legitimate and worthwhile.

Performance-based assessments generally do not yield a *single* correct answer or solution but allow for a wide range of responses. Thus, evaluations of student responses, products, and performances must be based on judgments. The evaluative judgments are guided by criteria that define the desired elements of quality (Ferrara, Goldberg, and McTighe 1995). One widely used scoring tool is a *rubric,* a scoring tool used to evaluate the quality of constructed-response products and performances. Rubrics consist of a fixed measurement scale (e.g., four-point) and a list of criteria that describe the characteristics for each score point. Rubrics are frequently accompanied by representative examples of student products or performances that illustrate each of the points on the scale. These examples are called *anchors.*

The term *standards* is frequently used in conjunction with performance-based assessments. There are three distinct ways in which the term is used: (1) *content standards*, which specify *what* students should know and be able to do; (2) *performance standards*, which set expectations about *how well* students should perform; and (3) *opportunity-to-learn* standards, having to do with the necessary *resources and conditions* for effective teaching and learning. Performance-based assessments call for decisions about content standards as well as expected standards for performance (Diez 1993). Three primary types of performance-based assessments are products, performances, and process-focused assessments.

Product. Student products provide tangible indicators of the application of knowledge and skills. Many educators believe that product assessment is especially "authentic" because it closely resembles real work outside of school. Teachers may evaluate *written products* (e.g., essays, research papers, laboratory reports), *visual products* (e.g., two- and three-dimensional models, displays, videotapes), *aural products* (e.g., an audiotape of an oral presentation), and other types of products to determine degrees of proficiency or levels of quality.

Product assessment calls for the selection or development of criteria for evaluation. The criteria are incorporated into a scoring rubric, rating scale, or checklist. Many teachers recognize that evaluation criteria also serve an instructional purpose: providing students with a clear focus on elements of quality to guide their work. When the criteria are made public, students may be involved in using them in peer- and self-evaluation of products.

One application of product assessment is systematically collecting representative samples of student work over time in portfolios. Portfolios allow teachers, students, parents, and others to observe development and growth in learning. Portfolio assessment has been widely used

> **Many teachers recognize that evaluation criteria also serve an instructional purpose: providing students with a clear focus on elements of quality to guide their work.**

CLASSROOM EXAMPLES

Students develop a computer program for an advanced high school computer class. Their teacher evaluates students' programming knowledge and skills by examining the program's written code for accuracy and efficiency. In addition, students must run the program to demonstrate that it performs the specified functions. Unsuccessful programs must be "debugged" until they satisfactorily fulfill the requirements.

A second grade teacher collects biweekly examples of representative student work in a language arts portfolio. The collected student samples are reviewed with parents during mid-year conferences. The portfolio provides parents with tangible illustrations of their child's literacy development. The teacher uses the actual products, along with a developmental scale of reading and writing for the primary grades, to discuss the student's skill strengths and point out areas needing special attention.

A college engineering professor assigns his students to work in teams to design and build a self-propelled hovering vehicle that corresponds to certain specified parameters. In addition to the model, students must individually prepare a technical report related to their design. The models and technical reports are evaluated to determine students' understanding of, and ability to apply, principles of aerodynamics. A culminating "hovering" contest is used to determine the most effective designs.

Fifth grade art students create a landscape using tempera paints. Using a skills checklist, their art teacher assesses their paintings to determine their proficiency in using the medium. He also assesses their understanding of the use of compositional elements for creating an illusion of depth. Individual student conferences are arranged to provide feedback.

A middle school science teacher reviews her students' laboratory reports to determine their effectiveness in applying experimental procedures and the accuracy of their data collection. Her written comments in the margins point out errors and offer specific suggestions for improvement. The reports are returned, discussed, and filed in the students' science folders for future reference.

over the years in the visual arts, architecture, and technical areas.

In recent years teachers have increasingly used portfolios to document learning in other subject areas, especially the language arts. For additional information on the use of portfolios in the classroom, see *Student Portfolios* (National Education Association 1993).

The use of products and portfolios can be appealing. When students are given opportunities to produce authentic products, they often become more engaged in, and committed to, their learning. Unlike standardized assessments that require uniform student responses, performance-based assessments in which students create a product allow students to express their individuality. Product assessments also indicate what students can do, while revealing what they need to learn or improve. When teachers share the criteria used to evaluate products, students know the elements of quality that will serve as a guide for peer- and self-evaluation. Previously developed products can serve an instructional purpose when they are presented as models of excellence for students (McTighe 1997; Wiggins 1992).

Despite their benefits, product assessments have their drawbacks. Criteria for judging the products must be identified, and product evaluation can be a time-consuming process. In addition, teachers must be careful when evaluating student products that their judgments are not unduly influenced by extraneous variables, such as neatness or spelling. Practicality must also be considered. The time required to develop quality products may compete with other instructional priorities. Product assessments require resources, including funds for materials and space for display and storage.

Performance. Using performance assessments, teachers are able to observe directly the application of desired skills and knowledge. Performance assessments are among the most authentic types of student assessments because they can replicate the kinds of actual performances occurring in the world outside of school. Performances have been used widely to assess learning in certain disciplines, such as vocal and instrumental music, physical education, speech, and theater, where performance is the natural focus of instruction. However, teachers in other subjects can include performances, such as oral presentations, demonstrations, and debates, as part of an array of assessment methods.

As with product assessments, teachers must develop criteria and scoring tools, such as rubrics, rating scales, or checklists, to evaluate student performances. Students gain additional instructional value when they apply the scoring tools for

CLASSROOM EXAMPLES

Students in the school orchestra participate in a dress rehearsal two weeks before the public performance. The music teacher works with the students to evaluate their performance during the rehearsal and identify areas of weakness. During the ensuing practices, the orchestra members concentrate on making improvements in these areas prior to the actual performance before a live audience.

A high school social studies teacher sets up an in-class debate as a culminating activity for a contemporary issues unit. Students work as part of a team to debate the issue of gun control. The teacher will rate students' performances in the debates on several dimensions including their understanding of the Bill of Rights, persuasiveness of their arguments, use of supporting factual information, effectiveness in countering rebuttals, and observance of rules of debating.

An elementary physical education teacher uses a skills checklist during the unit on introductory gymnastics to assess students' proficiency. Each student receives a copy of the checklist and works with a partner to try to successfully perform the identified skills. The completed checklists are used as one component of the culminating grade for the unit.

A high school speech teacher works with a home economics teacher in preparing students to make oral presentations to communicate the results of a nutrition research project. Using a rating scale, the home economics teacher evaluates the students on accuracy and completeness of their knowledge of the "food pyramid." The speech teacher uses a scoring rubric for delivery of an informative speech to evaluate the oral presentations.

CLASSROOM EXAMPLES

A high school literature teacher regularly poses oral questions to assess students' interpretation of a text. Their responses sometimes reveal misunderstandings that need clarification by the teacher.

A kindergarten teacher interviews each of her children in the beginning of the year. This informal assessment provides useful information about cognitive and linguistic development, social skills, and areas of personal interest.

A middle school social studies teacher carefully observes students to assess their cooperative skills as they work on a social studies project in learning groups. He also selects students to serve as process observers, giving them a checklist of observable indicators of cooperative skills. The teacher and student observers periodically provide feedback to the class on the effectiveness of their interactions in cooperative groups.

A high school mathematics teacher asks students to describe their reasoning processes by thinking out loud during the solution of open-ended problems. By listening to students as they articulate their thoughts, the teacher can identify fallacious reasoning and give feedback on the appropriateness of strategies they are using, thus providing needed assistance.

peer- and self-evaluation. Such involvement helps students to internalize the elements of quality embedded in the criteria. Many teachers have observed that students are motivated to put forth greater effort when they perform before "real" audiences of other students, staff, parents, or expert judges. Schools also benefit from positive public relations when students perform for the community.

Many teachers have observed that students are motivated to put forth greater effort when they perform before "real" audiences of other students, staff, parents, or expert judges.

Despite their positive features, performance assessments can be time- and labor-intensive for students and teachers. Time must be allocated for rehearsal as well as for the actual performances. The evaluation of performances is particularly susceptible to evaluator biases, making fair, valid, and reliable assessment a challenge.

Process-Focused Assessment. Process-focused assessments provide information on students' learning strategies and thinking processes. Rather than focusing on tangible

> Rather than focusing on tangible products or performances, [process-focused assessment] focuses on gaining insights into the underlying cognitive processes used by students.

products or performances, this approach focuses on gaining insights into the underlying cognitive processes used by students. A variety of process-focused assessments are routinely used as a natural part of teaching. For example, teachers may elicit students' thinking processes using oral questions such as: "How are these two things alike and different?" or by asking students to "think out loud" as they solve a problem or make a decision. Teachers may ask students to document their thinking over time by keeping a learning log. Also, teachers can learn about students' thinking processes by observing students as they function in the classroom. This "kid watching" method is especially well suited to assessing the development of attitudes or habits of mind, such as persistence.

Process-focused assessments are formative in that they provide diagnostic information to teachers and feedback to students. They may also support the development of students' metacognition by heightening their awareness of cognitive processes and worthwhile strategies. Process-focused assessment methods are typically used over time, rather than on single occasions. Thus, they are rarely used in standardized, high stakes evaluations of students.

V.

EVALUATION METHODS AND ROLES

In addition to making choices about classroom assessment methods, teachers should consider options for evaluating student work (see Figure 3).

One question teachers must ask is: "How will we evaluate student knowledge and proficiency?" They should determine evaluation methods largely by the assessment approach and the nature of the student responses to the assessment item or task. Selected-response format items and some brief constructed response items (e.g., fill in the blank) yield a single correct or best answer. Most often teachers score such items using a key with the answers. Sometimes they ask students to "bubble in" their answers on an answer sheet that can be scanned by machine or hand-scored by overlaying a scoring template. Scoring of selected-response format items is relatively quick, easy, and objective.

Assessments using constructed-response formats elicit a range of responses, products, or performances that reflect varying degrees of quality and different levels of proficiency. Because such assessments typically do not have a *single* correct answer, teachers must rely on judgment-based methods to evaluate responses to these open-ended assessments. Four primary types of evaluation methods are used with constructed-response formats: scoring rubrics, rating scales, checklists, and written and oral comments.

A *scoring rubric* consists of evaluative criteria, a fixed scale (e.g., four or six points), and descriptive terms for discriminating among different degrees of understanding, quality, or proficiency. The term *rubric* has its origins in the Latin word *rubrica,* meaning "red earth used to mark something of significance." Today, educators use *rubric* to communicate the important qualities in a product or performance.

Scoring rubrics can be *holistic* (providing an overall impression of the elements of quality and levels of performance in a student's work) or *analytic* (indicating the level of performance of a student's work on two or more separate traits). For example, the reading rubric in Figure 4 presents an example of a holistic rubric for evaluating reading comprehension. The oral presentation rubric in Figure 5 shows an analytic rubric for oral presentations. Notice that in the analytic rubric, four traits (content, organization, delivery, language conventions) are evaluated independently.

Figure 3

Evaluation and Communication Methods

Evaluation Method	Evaluation Role	Communication/Feedback Method
How will we evaluate student knowledge and proficiency?	*Who will be involved in the evaluation?*	*How will we communicate assessment results?*
Selected-Response Format*	**Evaluator**	**Presentation of Results**
☐ answer key	☐ teacher(s)/ instructor(s)	☐ numerical score
☐ scoring template	☐ peers	• percentage scores
☐ machine scoring	☐ expert judges (external raters)	• point totals
	☐ student (self-evaluation)	☐ letter grade
Constructed-Response Format	☐ parents/ community members	☐ parents
☐ scoring rubric	☐ other: _____	☐ developmental/proficiency scale
• generic		☐ rubric
• task-specific		☐ checklist
☐ bipolar rating scale		☐ written comments
☐ checklist		☐ narrative report (written)
☐ written/oral comments		☐ verbal report/ conference

*These evaluation methods may be used for some brief constructed response items (e.g., fill in the blank, short answer).

Figure 4 **Reading Rubric**	
Rating Scale	**Evaluative Criteria**
4	Reader displays a sophisticated understanding of the text with substantial evidence of constructing meaning. Multiple connections are made between the text and the reader's ideas/experiences. Interpretations are sophisticated and directly supported by appropriate text references. Reader explicitly takes a critical stance (e.g., analyzes the author's style, questions the text, provides alternate interpretations, views the text from multiple perspectives).
3	Reader displays a solid understanding of the text with clear evidence of constructing meaning. Connections are made between the text and the reader's ideas/experiences. Interpretations are made and generally supported by appropriate text references. Reader may reveal a critical stance toward the text.
2	Reader displays a partial understanding of the text with some evidence of constructing meaning. A connection may be made between the text and the reader's ideas/experiences, but it is not developed. Interpretations are not made and/or not supported by appropriate text references. Reader shows no evidence of a critical stance toward the text.
1	Reader displays a superficial understanding of the text with limited evidence of constructing meaning. No connections are made between the text and the reader's ideas/experiences. Reader provides no interpretations or evidence of a critical stance.
0	Reader displays no evidence of text comprehension or constructing meaning.

Holistic rubrics are most appropriately used for summative purposes (such as the evaluation provided at the conclusion of unit or a course) where the goal is to provide an overall picture of student performance. Most report card grades represent holistic evaluation, since a variety of "subscores" (tests, quizzes, performance tasks, homework, classwork, etc.) are collapsed into a single symbol—the letter grade—for each subject.

	Figure 5			
	Oral Presentation Rubric			
Rating Scale	**Evaluative Criteria**			
	Content	**Organization**	**Delivery**	**Language Conventions**
4	(Varies by assignment)	Coherent organization throughout; logical sequence; smooth transitions; effective introduction and conclusion	Excellent volume; fluent delivery with varied intonation; effective body language and eye contact	Highly effective use of language enhances the message; few, if any, grammatical mistakes
3	(Varies by assignment)	Good organization generally but with some break in the logical flow of ideas; clear transitions; identifiable introduction and conclusion	Adequate volume and intonation; generally fluent; generally effective body language and eye contact	Generally effective use of language supports the message; minor grammatical errors do not interfere with message
2	(Varies by assignment)	Flawed organization; ideas not developed; weak transitions; ineffective conclusion	Volume is too low or too loud; delivery is not fluent; body language and eye contact do not enhance message	Use of language not always aligned with the message; grammatical errors may interfere with message
1	(Varies by assignment)	Lack of organization; flow of ideas difficult to follow; no evidence of transitions; no introduction or conclusion	Message cannot be understood due to low volume; strained delivery; ineffective body language; lack of eye contact	Major grammatical errors make the message very difficult or impossible to follow

Holistic rubrics have their place, but teachers should employ primarily analytic rubrics for day-to-day evaluation in their classrooms. Since they identify and evaluate particular traits, analytic rubrics provide more detailed and specific feedback to students about the strengths of their performance and the areas needing attention. If

Figure 6 **Art Rubric**	
Rating Scale	**Evaluative Criteria**
3	Identifies three or more relevant differences between the work of Matisse and van Allsburg (e.g., use of color, level of detail/simplification, use of line and shape, materials, process) Identifies a preference for one artist's style Supports preference with two or more well-stated reasons citing specific examples from the artist's work Uses a variety of art vocabulary terms appropriately
2	Identifies two relevant differences between the work of Matisse and van Allsburg Identifies a preference for one artist's style Supports preference with one reason citing an example from the artist's work Uses one or two art vocabulary terms appropriately
I	Does not clearly identify significant differences between the work of Matisse and van Allsburg Identifies a preference for one artist's style, but does not support preference with reasons or examples Does not use art vocabulary terms appropriately

the goal is to improve student learning, not simply grade it, then such specific feedback is needed. How can students improve their research skills, for instance, if all they receive is a "3" on a holistic rubric (or a "B-" on a research report)? Such evaluations provide little meaningful guidance about how to do a better job in the future. An analytic rubric, on the other hand, offers greater specificity. For example, a student receiving the following descriptive comments on an analytic rubric— "uses several appropriate sources to gather information on the topic" and "needs to document all sources using standard bibliographic notation"—is informed about a strength of the research (use of multiple sources) and a weakness (lack of complete documentation). The intent of such feedback is to encourage the student to become more attentive to the importance of careful source documentation on future research projects.

Rather than choosing between these two types of rubrics, teachers can use both during a course or unit of study. They can use the analytic rubric(s) "along the way" to inform teaching and guide student practice and revision, and they can use the holistic rubric(s) at the conclusion of a performance task or unit assessment to provide an overall evaluation of student knowledge and proficiency.

In addition to being analytic or holistic, rubrics also may be *generic* or *task-specific*. A generic rubric provides general criteria for evaluating a student's performance in a given performance area. The rubrics shown in Figures 4 and 5 are generic rubrics since they may be used to evaluate a variety of responses to reading and oral presentations, respectively. In contrast, a task-specific rubric is designed for use with a particular assessment task. For example, the art rubric in Figure 6 presents a rubric used to assess the task of comparing the styles and techniques of two artists (Matisse and van Allsburg) and indicating a preference. Notice that a task-specific rubric, such as this one, cannot be used to evaluate responses to different performance tasks.

Generic rubrics offer the capability of multiple applications within a given area, such as mathematical problem solving, persuasive writing, and research. Rather than creating a new rubric for each and every performance task, the same rubric can be taught to students, posted in the room, and used throughout the year (and often across grade levels). With repeated use, the criteria contained in the generic rubric can be internalized by students so that they are better able to consider the qualities of effective performance *while* they are working, as well as to evaluate their own work when they are finished.

There are times, however, when a task-specific rubric will be preferable. For instance, task-specific rubrics tend to yield greater reliability (consistency) when used by different teachers. Thus, a department or grade-level team might employ a task-specific rubric for use with a common performance task or final exam given by more than one teacher. Task-specific rubrics can be customized from generic rubrics.

Rubrics are most effectively used for evaluation or instruction when they are accompanied by examples of responses for each score point. These examples or *anchors* provide tangible illustrations of the various points on the rating scale. Perhaps the greatest advantage of rubrics is their clear delineation of the elements of quality. They provide students with clear performance targets, expectations about what is most important, and criteria for evaluating and improving their own work. They provide teachers with specific criteria for reliably evaluating student responses, products, or performances; a "tool" for increasing the consistency of evaluation among teachers; and clear targets for instruction.

These evaluation methods require time to collect or develop rubrics, to identify representative anchors, to develop proficiency in applying them reliably, and to use them for evaluating student responses, products, and performances. Nonetheless, some schools and districts have recognized the significant professional development benefits of providing opportunities for teachers to work together on scoring student responses, products, and performances and identifying anchors.

Rating scales may also be used to evaluate responses to open-ended questions and tasks. *Bipolar rating scales* (see Figure 7), for example, are widely used on questionnaires and can be applied to educational assessments as well. Such a scale might be used in conjunction with evaluations related to program selection (e.g., special education placement) or for peer evaluation of a product or performance (e.g., "This oral presentation achieves its stated purpose.").

Checklists contain categories (i.e., specific features or dimensions) for evaluation and rating options for each category. The rating options may offer a simple "yes" or "no" to indicate the presence or absence of each dimension, or a narrow scale, such as "never," "rarely," or "frequently." Checklists are easy-to-use, efficient evaluation tools. They can be used while teaching a lesson or leading a discussion and are especially useful when observing students at work. Checklists may also be used as guides by students, individually or in groups, while they engage in performance activities.

> Some schools and districts have recognized the significant professional development benefits of providing opportunities for teachers to work together on scoring student responses, products, and performances and identifying anchors.

While rating scales and checklists are simple to apply in the classroom, they generally do not provide the detailed, explicit criteria found in rubrics. Thus, they are open to differing interpretations and greater subjectivity when used to evaluate student products and performances.

Written and oral comments can be effective in evaluating student work because they enable teachers to communicate clearly and directly with their students about elements of quality, expected standards of performance, areas of strengths, and needed improvements. These methods allow teachers to provide evaluative feedback to students on a personal level. Written and oral comments can require a great deal

Figure 7
Sample Bipolar Rating Scale

Scoring Criteria				
Strongly Disagree	Disagree	Not Sure	Agree	Strongly Agree
-2	-1	0	1	2

of teacher time and are especially demanding for secondary teachers working with one hundred or more students per day. The effectiveness of personal comments may be diminished if teachers provide only negative feedback (identifying errors or problems), make nonspecific positive comments that do not acknowledge particular aspects of student effort and work, or make comments that do not address all important elements of quality.

Teachers must also ask: "Who will be involved in the evaluation?" As always, this guiding question should be answered with content standards, purposes, audiences, and methods in mind. The question also brings to mind the opportunity to involve others in the evaluation process. Teachers may involve other staff members, parents, or community experts in the evaluation of student products (e.g., science fair projects) and performances (e.g., public-speaking exhibitions). They may also involve students. When students are engaged in applying criteria for self- and peer-evaluation, they begin to internalize elements of quality and performance standards in ways that can lead to improvements in the quality of their work and learning.

VI.

COMMUNICATION AND FEEDBACK METHODS

After evaluations are made, teachers must ask: "How will we communicate assessment results?" A variety of methods can be used, including numerical scores, letter grades, verbal and written reports, scales, and checklists (see Figure 3). The choice of communication methods should be determined by assessment purposes and methods, evaluation methods, and especially the audience for the assessment information.

Numerical scores (e.g., percentage correct or number of points earned on a classroom quiz) and *letter grades* are widely used methods for communicating the results of classroom assessments. Both methods are efficient to use and succinct, but numerical scores and grades, by themselves, do not explicitly communicate the elements of quality and standards of performance that they are meant to reflect. For example, saying that 70 percent correct is a "C" can mean one thing on an easy task and something different on a difficult task and it does not make clear what a student knows and can do. Likewise, when students are graded "on a curve," their knowledge or performance level is communicated in relation to other students in the class, not in terms of established criteria and standards.

> **The choice of communication methods should be determined by assessment purposes and methods, evaluation methods, and especially the audience for the assessment information.**

Developmental and proficiency scales are generally more informative than numerical scores and grades because they contain descriptions of different degrees of quality and levels of performance (see Figure 8 for an example of a developmental scale for reading). Information about student learning presented in terms of developmental or proficiency levels can be especially meaningful to parents. Recognizing this fact, some schools and districts have revised their report cards, especially for the primary grades, to incorporate features of developmental and proficiency scales.

Checklists can also be effective for communicating assessment results because they present ratings on identified criteria or elements of quality. They are a quick and efficient method for providing direct and timely feedback to students. However, checklist developers must be careful to avoid poorly defined categories, such as creativity, that are open to diverse interpretations.

Figure 8

Developmental Reading Scale

Emergent Reader
- ☐ follows along in the text when adult reads
- ☐ is aware of relationship of printed text to oral language
- ☐ uses picture cues when recalling story
- ☐ pretends to read; memorizes favorite stories

Beginner Reader
- ☐ reads word-for-word; struggles with unfamiliar material
- ☐ has limited sight vocabulary of one- and two-syllable words
- ☐ attempts to pronounce and figure out meaning of new words
- ☐ demonstrates comprehension of simple text
- ☐ occasionally monitors comprehension and self-corrects

Competent Reader
- ☐ reads familiar material comfortably
- ☐ has large sight vocabulary
- ☐ uses context clues to figure out meaning of unfamiliar words
- ☐ actively constructs meaning
- ☐ regularly monitors comprehension and self-corrects

Fluent Reader
- ☐ reads fluently with expression
- ☐ has extensive sight vocabulary
- ☐ readily determines meaning of unfamiliar words using context clues
- ☐ reads a wide variety of materials with understanding
- ☐ independently monitors comprehension; appropriately applies comprehension strategies

Written comments, narrative reports, verbal reports, and conferences can be effective communication methods because they provide opportunities to clearly and directly connect student effort and performance to elements of quality and standards of performance. They also allow teachers to provide more individualized and personal feedback than the other communication methods. Regrettably, the time-consuming nature of these methods often limits their use, especially for teachers at the secondary level because of the greater student-to-teacher ratio.

AFTERWORD

Assessment is an essential component of the teaching and learning process. Without effective classroom assessment, it is impossible for teachers to know whether students are "hitting the target"—that is, learning what is important for them to learn. However, the significance of classroom assessment extends beyond the role of measuring learning. What we assess, how we assess and evaluate, and how we communicate results send a clear message to students about what is worth learning, how it should be learned, what elements of quality are most important, and how well we expect them to perform. By considering the key questions and principles presented here, teachers will be better equipped to develop and use classroom assessments that provide fair, valid, and reliable information that will inform teaching and promote learning.

GLOSSARY

analytic scoring—scoring procedure in which responses, products, or performances are evaluated for selected dimensions, with each dimension receiving a separate score. For example, a piece of writing may be evaluated on several categories, such as organization, use of details, attention to audience, and language usage and mechanics. Analytic scores may be weighted and totaled.

anchor(s)—representative responses, products, or performances used to illustrate each point on a scoring scale. They are also referred to as "models" and "range-finder papers." Anchors for the highest score point are sometimes referred to as exemplars.

assessment—any systematic basis for making inferences about characteristics of people, usually based on various sources of evidence; the global process of synthesizing information about individuals in order to understand and describe them better (Brown 1983).

authentic assessment—refers to assessment tasks that evoke demonstrations of knowledge and skills in ways that they are applied in the "real world." Ideally, authentic assessment tasks also engage students and reflect best instructional activities. Thus, teaching to the task may be desirable.

content standard—a goal statement specifying desired knowledge, skills or processes, and attitudes to be developed as a result of educational experiences.

criteria—guidelines, rules, or principles by which student responses, products, or performances are evaluated.

criterion referenced—an approach for describing a student's performance on an assessment according to established criteria.

evaluation—judgment regarding the quality, value, or worth of a response, product, or performance based upon established criteria.

formative assessment—ongoing, diagnostic assessment providing information (feedback) to guide instruction and improve student performance.

generalizability—the extent to which responses, products, or performances sampled by a set of assessment activities are representative of the broader domain being assessed.

holistic scoring—a scoring procedure yielding a single score based upon an overall impression of a response, product, or performance.

indicator—a specific description of an outcome in terms of observable and assessable behaviors. An indicator specifies what a person who possesses the qualities articulated in a content standard knows or can do. Generally, several indicators are needed to adequately describe each content standard.

interdisciplinary or **integrated assessment**—assessment that uses tasks that test students' abilities to apply concepts, principles, skills, and processes from two or more subject disciplines to a central question, theme, issue, or problem.

norm referenced—an approach for describing a student's performance on an assessment by comparison to a norm group.

opportunity-to-learn standards—the conditions and resources necessary for teachers and schools to meet higher standards for students.

performance-based assessment (or **performance assessment**)—an assessment activity that requires students to construct a response, create a product, or perform a demonstration. Performance-based assessments generally do not yield a *single* correct answer or solution but allow for a wider range of responses. Thus, evaluations of student responses, products, and performances are based on judgments guided by criteria.

performance standard—an established level of achievement, quality, or proficiency. Performance standards set expectations about how much students should know and how well students should perform.

performance task—an assessment activity, or set of activities, related to one or more content standards, that elicits one or more responses to a question or problem.

portfolio—a purposeful, integrated collection of student work showing effort, progress, or achievement in one or more areas (adapted from Paulson, Paulson, and Meyer 1991). Since they feature works selected over time, portfolios are well suited to assess student growth and development.

primary trait(s) scoring—a scoring procedure in which responses, products, or performances are evaluated by limiting attention to a single criterion. These individual criteria are based upon the trait determined to be essential for a successful performance on a given task. For example, persuasiveness might be the primary trait being evaluated in a note to a principal urging a change in a school rule. Scorers would attend only to that trait.

proficiency—having or demonstrating a high degree of knowledge or skill in a particular area.

reliability—the degree to which an assessment yields dependable and consistent results.

rubric—a scoring tool used to evaluate a student's performance in a content area. Rubrics consist of a fixed measurement scale (e.g., a four-point scale) and a list of criteria that describe the characteristics of products or performances for each score point. Rubrics are frequently accompanied by examples (anchors) of student responses, products, or performances to illustrate each of the points on the scale.

standardized assessment—an assessment that uses a set of consistent procedures for constructing, administering, and scoring. The goal of standardization is to ensure that all students are assessed under uniform conditions so that interpretation of their performance is comparable and not influenced by differing conditions (Brown 1983).

summative assessment—culminating assessment for a unit, grade level, or course of study providing a status report on mastery or degree of proficiency according to identified content standards.

test—a set of questions or situations designed to elicit responses that permit an inference about what a student knows or can do. Tests generally utilize a paper-and-pencil format, occur within established time limits, restrict access to resources (e.g., reference materials), and yield a limited range of acceptable responses.

validity—refers to the degree to which an assessment measures what it is intended to measure.

REFERENCES

Airasian, P.W. 1997. *Classroom assessment.* 3rd ed. New York: McGraw-Hill.

Brown, F.G. 1983. *Principles of educational and psychological testing.* 3rd ed. New York: Holt, Rinehart and Winston.

Carlson, S.B. 1985. *Creative classroom testing: 10 designs for assessment and instruction.* Princeton, N.J.: Educational Testing Service.

Cross, K.P., and T.A. Angelo. 1988. *Classroom assessment techniques: A handbook for faculty.* (Technical Report No. 88-A-004.0). Ann Arbor, Mich.: University of Michigan, National Center for Research to Improve Postsecondary Teaching and Learning.

Diez, M. 1993. *Essays on emerging assessment issues.* Washington, D.C.: American Association of Colleges for Teacher Education.

Ferrara, S., G. Goldberg, and J. McTighe. 1995. *Ways in which teachers communicate learning targets, criteria, and standards for performance to their students.* Paper presented at the annual meeting of the American Educational Research Association, San Francisco.

Ferrara, S., and J. McTighe. 1992. Assessment: a thoughtful process. In *If minds matter: A foreword to the future.* Vol. 2. Palatine, Ill.: Skylight Publishing.

Haladyna, T.M. 1994. *Developing and validating multiple-choice test items.* Hillsdale, N.J.: Lawrence Erlbaum Associates.

Herman, J.L., P.R. Aschbacher, and L. Winters. 1992. *A practical guide to alternative assessment.* Alexandria, Va.: Association for Supervision and Curriculum Development.

Marzano, R., D. Pickering, and J. McTighe. 1993. *Assessing outcomes: Performance assessment using dimensions of learning.* Alexandria, Va.: Association for Supervision and Curriculum Development.

McTighe, J. 1997. What happens between assessments? *Educational Leadership* 54(4): 6-12.

Mitchell, R. 1992. *Testing for learning: How new approaches to evaluation can improve America's schools*. New York: The Free Press.

Mitchell, R., and M. Neill. 1992. *Criteria for evaluation of student assessment systems*. Washington, D.C.: National Forum on Assessment.

National Education Association. 1993. *Student portfolios*. Washington, D.C.: NEA Professional Library.

Nitko, A.J. 1983. *Educational tests and measurement: An introduction*. New York: Harcourt Brace Jovanovich.

Paulson, F.L., P.R. Paulson, and C.A. Meyer. 1991. What makes a portfolio a portfolio? *Educational Leadership* 48(5): 60-63.

Perrone, V., ed. 1991. *Expanding student assessment*. Alexandria, Va.: Association for Supervision and Curriculum Development.

Shepard, L. 1989. Why we need better assessments. *Educational Leadership* 46(7): 4-9.

Smith, M.L. 1993. *The role of high-stakes testing in school reform*. Washington, D.C.: National Education Association.

Stiggins, R.J. 1997. *Student-centered classroom assessment*. 2nd ed. New York: Macmillan College Publishing Company.

Stiggins, R.J., and N.F. Conklin. 1992. *In teachers' hands: Investigating the practices of classroom assessment*. Albany, N.Y.: State University of New York Press.

Wiggins, G.P. 1989. Teaching to the (authentic) test. *Educational Leadership* 46(7): 41-47.

———. 1992. Standards, not standardization: Evoking quality student work. *Educational Leadership* 4(5): 18-25.